Victoria

The ART of
FLOWERS

Victoria

The ART of
FLOWERS

FROM THE EDITORS OF *VICTORIA*

83
PRESS

Hoffman Media
1900 International Park Drive, Suite 50
Birmingham, Alabama 35243
hoffmanmedia.com

ISBN 978-1-940772-87-5
Printed in China

83
PRESS

CONTENTS

INTRODUCTION

L ONG BEFORE THE FIRST BLOSSOMS come into view, a symphony of scents stirs the air in a redolent greeting. An arched trellis, scarcely visible beneath an outpouring of roses, opens to a path lined with lacy hydrangeas, cape jasmine, and sweet oleander. The anticipation of what lies ahead is almost as heady as the aroma of the blooms themselves, and then the full garden emerges in a scene so beautiful it takes one's breath away.

Flowers do more than bring color and fragrance—they offer sustenance for the soul. Just a whisper of the citrusy scent of a peony or a glimpse of a pansy's cheerful face can stir up tender memories in the heart of the beholder. Gardeners know the simple satisfaction of caring for delicate seedlings and watching them grow, much like a mother lovingly raises her children. And just like children, plants benefit from encouragement, a guiding hand, and plenty of sunshine.

The pages of *Victoria* magazine brim with flowers. From blissful backyard beds to extravagant formal plots and from elaborate centerpieces for special occasions to petite posies to brighten a dreary day, we love them in all their glorious forms. That is why we are so pleased to present this inspiring volume of floral pageantry. So, turn the page and step into our garden—we'll be waiting for you!

Scents
— AND —
SENSIBILITY

Adored for their beauty and bewitching scents, roses remain the most loved of flowers, joining other favorite blooms as must-haves for any garden.

The rose reigns supreme as queen of all flowers in the garden and in the hearts of gardeners everywhere. It is easy to see why. The alluring charms of roses give credence to their regal stature. Graceful and glamorous, they perform as well as they please, repudiating their reputation as demanding plants.

With informed choices and basic care, there's a rose to crown any garden. Heirloom roses defy age; having withstood the elements throughout generations, they possess a tough, versatile nature. Modern varieties offer the enhanced qualities of refined breeding and just keep getting better.

Delight may begin with roses, but passion also extends to a brilliant bouquet of other petal-perfect blossoms. Go ahead—take a whiff. Join in the world's love affair with the most magnificent of blooms.

Sumptuous
ROSES

Explore a vast array of rose varieties, including time-tested beauties that would have thrived in Grandmother's garden, as well as modern breeds developed for easy care. You'll find ideal options for almost any location among the range of beautifully blooming possibilities, from petite miniatures to massive climbers and other types. Narrow your choices by identifying some of the roses that grow best in your region, and then select the optimal locations for them in your garden.

Many gardeners choose roses on the basis of bloom color. Although this is mostly a matter of personal preference, also consider hues that will complement the existing palette in your garden.

> *"A PROFUSION
> OF PINK ROSES BENDING
> RAGGED IN THE
> RAIN SPEAKS TO ME
> OF ALL GENTLENESS AND
> ITS ENDURING."*
> —William Carlos Williams

CLIMBER: For dramatic effect, the long, arching canes of these vigorous growers can be guided to ascend fences, scale walls, and twine over arbors, pergolas, and trellises.

FLORIBUNDA: These bushy 2- to 4-foot-tall plants put on a summer-long show of flowers in abundant, colorful clusters. Plant them in beds or borders, and see why they are so popular—especially in smaller gardens.

HYBRID TEA: A single, perfectly elegant blossom on a long stem distinguishes the most widely grown of all roses. Choose from among more than ten thousand types of hybrid tea roses. They bloom repeatedly throughout the growing season and provide fabulous cut flowers.

GRANDIFLORA: These gracious shrubs reach 4 to 6 feet tall, exhibiting the best traits of both their parents: the hardiness, ongoing blooms, and clustered petals of floribundas and the classic form of hybrid teas. Grandifloras are also valued for their disease resistance and their stature as background plants in the garden.

MINIATURE: Beloved for their petite charms, plants in this assortment range from 6 inches to 6 feet tall. Their miniature flowers and leaves grow in proportion to the plant. Most are just right for small spaces, edging beds, or accent containers.

A *Rose*
IS A ROSE

Roses are shrubs, so it helps to keep this in mind when adding them to your garden. Like most shrubs, they grow quickly and can be used to help solve a range of common landscape problems, from creating a privacy screen to softening a hard structure, covering a slope, or adding lasting color. Many rose species are tough, long-lived plants that require minimal care.

Visit a nursery or a public garden during the bloom season, from late spring to late summer, to see which roses appeal to you most. Take notes and list favorites to help you plan your garden.

OLD GARDEN: Heirloom roses adapt to many landscape uses, as well as to extreme climates. Tried-and-true varieties boast blooms with luxuriant, soft-colored petals and exquisite fragrances. Each group within this impressive realm—'Alba', 'Bourbon', 'Centifolia', 'China', 'Damask', Hybrid Perpetual, 'Moss', 'Noisette', 'Portland', species, tea—includes prospects for you to treasure in your garden.

SHRUB: Outstanding among modern roses, this continually growing selection takes various forms, from neat bushes with small clusters of long-lasting flowers to tall arching and sprawling plants. Easy-care shrub roses work well in hedges.

SPECIES: As native wild plants from around the world, these drought-tolerant and disease-resistant roses typically survive in difficult conditions. Suited to informal naturalistic gardens, species roses display fall fruits called hips that both birds and people relish. Belonging to the same family as apples and crab apples, rose hips have a tart flavor and also contain high levels of vitamin C. They are used often in herbal teas, jams, and jellies.

Each rose has its own personality—bold, independent, and thorny or demure, delicate, and serene. Large flowers speak out. Others cluster colorfully or make simple, single-petal statements.

From the garden to a vase, roses please us endlessly with their aromatic charms. A rose's scent depends upon its lineage. Some have no perfume, while others possess a strong, enthralling redolence. Fragrances vary from sweet to spicy, fruity, musky, and more.

WITH TENDER CARE

Growing roses is easier than you might imagine. The key to healthy, fuss-free blooms comes with a little forethought before planting and a focus on prevention after you've added a rosebush to your garden. Use these tips to guide your rose-gardening success:

1 Choose sturdy, proven varieties. You'll find plenty of versatile and resilient shrubs appropriate for your climate, as well as for the conditions in your garden.

2 When adding a rosebush to your garden, give it plenty of room to grow and reach mature size.

3 Plant roses where they will receive at least six hours of direct sunlight daily. All-day sun is best.

4 Dig a planting hole twice as wide and just as deep as the nursery pot or root mass of your new plant.

5 Roses thrive in enriched soil. Improve soil before or after planting with several shovelfuls of composted manure worked into the area around the plant.

6 Feed plants monthly with rose fertilizer during the growing season. Stop feeding by late summer to avoid promoting tender new growth that could be damaged in later months by freezing weather.

7 Water roses weekly if nature doesn't provide soaking rains. Always water after fertilizing. Preserve soil moisture by spreading a 2-inch layer of mulch (compost, shredded leaves, and chopped bark) on the ground around the base of the plant.

8 Keeping plants healthy helps prevent both pests and diseases. Pausing frequently to enjoy your roses enables you to spot the first signs of problems. Take a nonchemical approach to troubleshooting: A blast with the garden hose often eliminates insect pests. Cleaning up leaf litter minimizes diseases.

9 Snipping off spent flowers keeps roses growing strong. Stop cutting by late summer to help plants slow their growth and prepare for winter. In late winter or early spring, trim off any damaged canes (stems). Remove brown canes that show no signs of life when the rest of the bush appears green.

10 If you live in a cold climate, help your roses survive by covering the base of each plant with compost heaped to 12 inches. In spring, uncover the plant when it begins to show new growth.

Give roses at least three years to become fully established in your garden. If the plant thrives, savor your success. If it doesn't, replace that rose with a different variety, and try again in another part of the garden.

GATHER YE BLOOMS

Discover the pleasures of roses beyond the garden. Savor the beauty and fragrance of rose petals, whether fresh or dried, by using them in various ways. Transform the exquisite petals of cut blossoms into numerous delights, from luxurious baths to sweet-smelling accents. Or capture the petals' irresistible scent by drying them for use long after their peak growing season.

Freeze fresh petals in ice cubes, and serve as a pretty garnish for herb teas and fruit drinks. (Use organically grown flowers only—not florist roses.) Sprinkle petals into a steaming bath, and bask in the delicate fragrance as you soak. (Scoop up the petals before draining the tub.) Toss a handful on your sweetheart's pillow as a way to say, "I love you."

Rose petals dry easily once removed from the plant and placed in an airy environment away from light and heat. To use dried petals in sweet-scented sachets, tie perfume-spritzed petals into a hankie, and tuck the sachet into a linen closet or a dresser drawer. Or use dried petals as packing material for a romantic gift.

Bridal Shower

✓ choose date
✓ mail invitations
✓ plan menu
  choose flowers
  buy gift
  confirm venue

Gracious and timeless, roses bring with them an unmistakable gentility and Old-World style unsurpassed by any other flower. Blissfully fragrant and utterly captivating, these magnificent blooms have been charming both romantics and gardening enthusiasts for centuries.

Ideal for an alfresco spring luncheon, a delicate rose motif conveys ageless beauty and enduring style. The perfect complement to Mother Nature's fresh green palette, a table draped in pristine white linen is topped with cloth napkins adorned with pink tea roses and stitched edges. Timeworn serving pieces in whisper-soft neutrals and posies of fresh blossoms emanate effortless ease and capture the essence of an idyllic afternoon.

Pampering Petals

Always take time to stop and smell the roses. Indulge in the romanticism of this most ubiquitous bloom by experimenting with a variety of petals. Your local garden center can recommend the most fragrant selections.

No need to splurge when you can make your own simple spa delicacies. Light a candle, cue soothing music, and experience some of nature's floral gifts by adding a rosy touch to these at-home beauty regimens. Prepare a cooling splash, a luxurious jar of powder, or a delightful footbath for houseguests, girlfriends, and, of course, your own sweet self. Relax, enjoy, and slip away into a rhapsody of roses.

"SWEET SPRING, FULL OF SWEET DAYS AND ROSES, A BOX WHERE SWEETS COMPACTED LIE."

—George Herbert

Enchanting WISTERIA

Whether cultivated to festoon the eaves of a stately manor, allowed to twine a wooden fence along a country lane, or gathered into fresh arrangements, wisteria offers languid beauty wherever it is found.

When wisteria reaches the peak of radiance—from late spring to early summer in most regions—let its lush cascades and intoxicating fragrance inspire a memorable celebration. Below right: The simple pleasure of indulging in a frosty treat befits a setting arrayed with seasonal bounty. Fostoria glassware in the Wisteria pattern calls attention to the featured bloom, while scoops of ice cream echo the hue of pink parrot tulips. Above left: Demure buds accent a Vista Alegre Viana footed teacup, saucer, and accent plate paired with a Wedgwood dinner plate.

Gently drooping petals lend gracious appeal to elegant centerpieces. Despite the plant's hardiness in its natural environment, as shown above left and below right, special care must be taken once it has been cut. Splitting woody stems, untangling blossoms, and removing most of the foliage will allow for better water absorption. Taking these extra measures will extend the life of an arrangement to a week or more. Below left and opposite: Soften mixed bouquets of vibrant blooms with the peaceful presence of wisteria. This page, above right: If any of the fragile tendrils break, showcase their delicate charm in posies.

Graceful
TULIPS

The tasteful drooping of a tulip suggests that there is elegance in rest. While spring is known for productivity, only relaxation and quietude give room to a blossoming imagination, inspiring beautiful tableaux and décor worthy of the season.

The tulip's soft stem presents a challenge to the perfectionist. However, for anyone willing to let the flowers arrange themselves, this bloom grants abundant ease. Opposite: A vase with little complexity offers the best complement to the simple blossom. Choose a container with ample depth to support the stem, and add a shallow amount of water. Trim each end with a sharp knife at a 45-degree angle, and remove leaves below the water line. Placed in the vessel, this display becomes an ideal centerpiece.

A hanging wreath dangles from blush and bashful ribbons. While the cabbage tulips, bridal wreath spirea, and hoary stock in shades of white and lavender slip easily between the branches of a grape vine frame, the look will last significantly longer when placed in soaked floral foam. Support this heavier chandelier with rope or wire hidden beneath the streamers. Opposite: As a favor for each guest, present a small bundle of florets, known as a "tussie-mussie," popularized during Queen Victoria's reign.

Luscious PEONIES

Peonies are aristocratic plants. In China, where they have been an important artistic symbol for centuries, they are called "the most beautiful" and connote riches and honor. In floral sanctuaries around the globe, these exuberant blooms are favored for their ruffly petals, gorgeous colors, and intoxicating aromas.

Like rare porcelain, sculptured peony blossoms are living works of art adorning gardens in May and June. Different species are native to Asia, southern Europe, and western North America. The plants flourish in USDA Zones 3 through 8, because they need winter chilling. Once established in a garden, peonies can live as long as fifty to one hundred years, becoming heritage plants to treasure for generations to come. Some Chinese peonies are very fragrant, with flower forms including hundred-petal, single, rose, and crown.

> ## *"THE PEONY WAS UNCHASTE, DISHEVELLED AS PEONIES MUST BE, AND AT THE HEIGHT OF ITS BEAUTY."*
> —Robertson Davies

There are two main categories of peonies: woody and herbaceous. The woody type can grow up to seven feet tall, while herbaceous varieties are smaller, growing up to six feet high and dying back each winter. Above: A sprawling tree stands sentinel in the foreground of this Pennsylvania property. Native oaks and maples provide a sheltered enclosure for mother plants. Below left: A giant swallowtail butterfly sips nectar from a 'Phoenix Purple' peony.

Bold, Beautiful
HYDRANGEAS

Widely acclaimed for their striking colors and showy blossoms, hydrangeas welcome summer with signature billowy blooms. Flowering forth in oversize clusters of blue, pink, green, and white, they epitomize a blissful, carefree temperament.

As mysterious as they are eye-catching, big-leaf hydrangeas have the ability to change color, depending upon the environment in which they grow—blue if aluminum is present in the soil; pink if they are deprived of aluminum. The 'Mophead' species, above left and above right, can often be revived by cutting the stems again and soaking wilted blooms in tepid water. In contrast to this flamboyant variety, 'Lacecap' hydrangeas, opposite and center left, exude a wispy, feminine mystique with their spare and graceful composure.

Whether dried in a basket or with their petals pressed into paper, hydrangeas possess an enduring loveliness with each incarnation. Steeped in nostalgia, our first recollection of them perhaps stems from a childhood memory. Wasn't there something innately magical about the sheer existence of this bloom—the whimsical shape, the unbelievable size, the hundreds of petals that could be tossed like confetti as we reveled in summer vacation?

Dramatic
DAHLIAS

*With their diversity of spectacular blooms
in summer gardens and cut-flower
displays, dahlias achieve what few other
plants can. Growing from humble tubers,
they put on a petal-powered show in
vibrant and pastel hues.*

Thousands of varieties tempt gardeners to select shapes, colors, and sizes ranging from spherical two-inch pompons to dinner plate–diameter stunners. Laciniated petals give a fringed look to this showy 'Nenekazi' blossom.

Just as summer reaches its sizzling peak and many plants fizzle, dahlias rise and shine, flowering until the first frost. The plants vary from compact to towering. Smaller specimens grow well in containers. Dahlias also intermingle beautifully with other floral companions, such as zinnias. Below right: Rebar is used to stake the giant stalks in this raised bed.

A *Profusion* OF FLOWERS

Seeming to grow beyond their garden borders, trailing vines wind their way into the home, lending natural beauty to petal-strewn fabrics and wallpapers, china patterns, and creative projects. These decorative elements infuse interiors with undeniable charm.

Opposite: A fresh bouquet draws the eye to this lovely vignette, where a floral focus unites a collection of plates of different sizes and from various makers. To create a similar display, arrange the grouping on a flat surface to determine a pleasing balance before hanging. This page: Pressed botanicals from artisan Anne Blackwell Thomspon preserve the ephemeral beauty of fresh blooms, above left, while Taylor Linens aprons evoke the cozy feel of a quaint English cottage, below right.

WHERE *Love* GROWS

It's late spring on Prince Edward Island, and all of nature seems to be joined in a floral jubilee of color and scent. Not far from where author Lucy Maud Montgomery set the beloved book series, Anne of Green Gables, *a gardener weaves her own story in halcyon surroundings.*

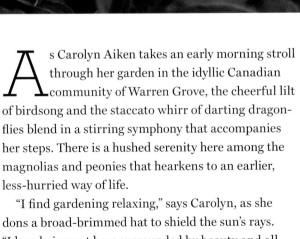

As Carolyn Aiken takes an early morning stroll through her garden in the idyllic Canadian community of Warren Grove, the cheerful lilt of birdsong and the staccato whirr of darting dragonflies blend in a stirring symphony that accompanies her steps. There is a hushed serenity here among the magnolias and peonies that hearkens to an earlier, less-hurried way of life.

"I find gardening relaxing," says Carolyn, as she dons a broad-brimmed hat to shield the sun's rays. "I love being out here surrounded by beauty and all the sights, sounds, and fragrances of nature." The 100-year-old farmhouse—where she and her husband, Andrew, raised their seven children—sits amid 10 peaceful acres, with a meandering brook and a large pond completing the rustic scene. It's close to the city but feels miles away from the bustling pace.

In the lush, flower-filled gardens, the Aikens share duties—with a little help from one of their sons—and count May and June as the busiest months of the year. They have more than forty lilac bushes, laden with sweet-scented purple blossoms, planted alongside deutzias, pretty shrubs in the same family as hydrangeas. Irises, roses, clematis, delphiniums, and daylilies are among the other botanical offerings the couple grow and groom to perfection. Andrew built the arbors and fences, as well as a blue-shutter-clad shed, one of several bespoke ornaments that lend enchantment to the surroundings.

The farmhouse has a relaxed, homey ambiance, with many of the furnishings found at antiques shops, thrift stores, and yard sales, and given new life with fresh coats of paint. Two other structures on the property, christened The Gardener's Cottage and The Boathouse, are built primarily of reclaimed materials and offer additional living and entertaining spaces.

With her grandchildren's laughter floating up from the pond and butterflies flitting among the daffodils and bluebells, Carolyn pauses to appreciate the tranquility she and her family enjoy here on Prince Edward Island. Through her blog, titled simply *Aiken House & Gardens*, she shares snippets of this inspiring pastoral life, one she is ever grateful to experience.

"My husband and I are both homebodies, and we have been blessed to have the space to create and enjoy the things we love," she says. "When we walk in our yard, it is always with a feeling of home sweet home!"

A Gardener's PALETTE

Become immersed in nature's prismatic array of hues. From snowy whites and soothing blues to a range of exuberant pinks and yellows, these spectacular colors paint a lovely and harmonious living portrait.

Like a painter's canvas, a garden comes to life with inspired imagination executed with artful brushstrokes of color. Paint a glorious picture in your landscape with harmonious blends of flowers and foliage. Whether you want to create a vivacious border of blooming delights or a restful backyard retreat, color sets the mood. Tranquility takes flight in a garden of white and green, while saturated shades of pink and purple set a more vibrant stage. If you're drawn to a particular type of flower, let it be the muse when devising a palette for your garden portrait. The many hues of Mother Nature offer a multitude of wondrous possibilities.

Variations ON A THEME

Feature favorite hues in the garden.

From one to another, carefully composed havens can be every bit as alluring, whether dressed in a riot of color, designed to highlight either complementary or contrasting values, or tightly focused around beloved monochromatic shades. When it comes to determining a pleasing and appropriate palette for the landscape, beauty is truly in the eye of the beholder. Choosing blossoms that will thrive in your climate and soil, develop a scheme that reflects your tastes.

Clockwise from above left: Pairing purple with a neighboring shade on the color wheel creates analogous charm, while setting the royal hue against its opposite provides a dynamic contrast. Pinks can range from gentle blush to deep fuchsia.

> *"THE GREATEST*
> *GIFT OF THE GARDEN IS*
> *THE RESTORATION OF*
> *THE FIVE SENSES."*
> —Hanna Rion

In the absence of marked color contrasts, bloom shapes and textures take center stage. To create a multidimensional composition, spotlight an assortment of flowers within the same color family and incorporate plants of varying heights and shapes. For example, the stately spires of purple delphiniums weave a rich tapestry of textures when combined with the shorter spikes of English lavender and the plump rosettes of violet dahlias.

Regardless of the hue you choose, green is a soothing constant, unifying surrounding shades with the greater landscape. Don't overlook the power of foliage plants, such as ferns, hostas, and coral bells, when creating your one-color oasis. Some, like coleus, even boast showy gradations of tones. When unfurling ribbons of color, consider pink, purple, yellow, and white.

Pink

From soft blush to nearly red, pink spans a range of colors. Roses alone offer an amazing array of petal-soft tints. To ensure a continual show of flowering beauty, plant camellias for winter romance, lovely peonies and tulips for spring enchantment, hydrangeas for an exuberant summer show, and mums for a colorful encore come fall.

Purple

The cool tones of heavenly hues from blue to purple not only enhance a garden's charm but also visually expand the sense of space. Whether you favor large, abundant blossoms, slender stems, or petite blooms, you can find flowers in the perfect color among many shades— periwinkle to deep violet, and even a true blue. Consider allium, clematis, delphiniums, salvia, and bellflowers.

Yellow

This naturally cheerful color brightens the landscape— especially in spring. Many early risers, such as daffodils, crocus, and forsythia, are known for their sunny hues. As summer approaches, opt for softer selections over vivid ones that can wash out in harsher light. Buttery yellow coreopsis and daylilies, for example, shine radiantly in a midsummer garden.

White

Beauties in this luminous color cast an ethereal glow over the garden by day and in the moonlight, too. Classic choices include lily of the valley, Shasta daisies, sweet autumn clematis, and butterfly bush. Light, airy flowers pair well with silver and gray foliage charmers, such as artemisia, lavender, and lamb's ears. Some white bloomers—jasmine, freesia, and gardenia—offer the added bonus of a sweet fragrance.

PERFECT PAIRINGS

Decorate the garden with harmonious color combinations.

A pleasing palette of blooms is the key to striking a melodious chord in the garden. The resulting symphony of color can be as subtle or as show-stopping as you envision.

Nothing lights up a landscape like a sea of flowers awash in bold hues. The pairing of complementary colors, which are opposite each other on the art world's color wheel, creates the most stunning of contrasts. One such combination is sunny yellow set against deep violet. Picture a dramatic duet of velvety purple iris and buttercream-colored columbine or ravishing red daylilies and lime-green gladiolus. The rich tone of the darker partner intensifies the brightness of the lighter one. Vibrant duos like these are a great way to energize garden features such as arbors, trellises, or containers.

Although a high-contrast landscape dazzles the eye through drama, cool combinations such as blue and white or gray and muted pink do so in an understated way. The result is a calming effect that soothes the soul. A fountain or a birdbath invigorates the eye, as well as the ear, when rimmed with soft pink blooms that echo the tranquil nature of the water within.

Cool hues, such as pastels and blue, recede visually, creating the illusion of a much larger space. They work wonders for making a cramped backyard or border look deeper. White flowers, in particular, exude a magical quality—perfect for lighting up shady pockets of the garden. Low-growing white bloomers, such as impatiens or alyssum, are ideal for lining a path because they will naturally illuminate it in the dark.

"GARDENING IS THE ART THAT USES FLOWERS AND PLANTS AS PAINT, AND THE SOIL AND SKY AS CANVAS."
—Elizabeth Murray

Uncontainable
BEAUTY

*Some horticulturalists are blessed to reside
near rolling hills or wide expanses with access
to ample space for cultivating a vision of
blossoms through which to stroll. For those
with a more limited canvas, there is hope
in the form of container gardening.*

Balconies may not be the first image in one's mind when visualizing a flourishing garden, but even the most urban locales can house cascading greenery and bountiful blooms. Using containers, growers can add versatility to larger beds or nurture vibrant flora on an otherwise barren surface.

The first step to creating a container garden is selecting a vessel. Various shapes and sizes can be used, but keep in mind the capsule's capacity, color, and design, among other features. Beginning gardeners may find success using larger pots that are less likely to dry out between waterings. When choosing the pot's material, consider where it will be located, as windowsills, for example, may have a weight limit. Also note how well the receptacle conducts heat, as greater temperature fluctuation can damage flowers. Wood and lightly hued surfaces help minimize this factor. Before planting, ensure the presence of a drainage hole at the base.

When arranging vegetation within the canister, one method is to incorporate a "thriller, filler, and spiller." The first is a focal point, typically tall and colorful to draw the eye. Plants with smaller leaves and flowers brim from the center, adding depth; it is best to choose varieties that continue to produce blooms faithfully throughout the season. Finally, a cascading vine is placed at the edge, where it can meander down, softening the bowl's appearance. Together, these three elements create a visually engaging array.

Gleanings
FROM
THE GARDEN

*With countless varieties just
waiting to be plucked, farmer-florist
Erin Benzakein strolls through her flower
beds in search of the perfect components to
create coveted arrangements.*

As anyone with a passion for gardening knows, the heart-stirring need to turn the soil, tuck in seeds, and tenderly nurture each sprout must be indulged. For Erin Benzakein, that yearning began with a 2-acre plot of land and a big dream that has blossomed into a thriving business, christened simply Floret.

Both a farm and a floral-design studio, Floret has drawn the attention of growers and consumers alike who support the local flower renaissance taking place around the globe. Erin's husband and two children work alongside her, making it a true family affair. With her quick success, this Washington State resident once contemplated expanding to a larger plot of land. "As we explored increasing our footprint, something just didn't sit right," she says. "Bigger isn't always better. So instead, we decided to hone our craft and focus our attention on perfecting the fine art of small-scale, high-intensity flower production."

Dahlias have always held sway in Erin's compact garden. Remarkably complex, they are actually composed of many individual flowers called florets—which makes them particularly appropriate for this eponymous venture. The entrepreneur started with just a few tubers a friend had given her, but the versatile blooms quickly became one of her favorites. She now cultivates more than four thousand dahlia plants among the crowded rows of sweet peas, zinnias, and other selections that make up the business's sizable inventory.

Dahlias, which are native to Mexico, boast more than forty varieties, ranging from petite to dinner plate–size, and can be found in every color but true blue. Erin believes the flowers are a wonderful addition to any late-summer bouquet, as they present countless design possibilities.

With hundreds of weddings and other special events in her portfolio, Erin generously shares her expertise at workshops, on her blog, and in beautifully photographed books. For this former *Victoria* Artist-in-Residence, inspiration still begins and ends in the garden. "I pay close attention to how the plants are growing in their natural habitat and then mimic that in the vase," she says. "Arching stems, scrambling vines, movement, and wildness are all key ingredients in every bouquet."

To replicate the arrangement below, you will need the following:

1. Geranium leaves
2. Lemon verbena
3. Love in a puff vines
4. Seven-son flowers
5. 'Platinum Blonde' dahlias
6. 'Cafe au Lait' dahlias
7. 'Kathryn Morley' roses
8. Scabiosa yellow zinnias
9. Collarette dahlias
10. Feverfew

Step-by-Step

Erin shares her instructions for assembling this pretty springtime bouquet.

1. Establish the shape of the arrangement by using different types of foliage. Geranium leaves and lemon verbena form a lush framework.

2. Add textural elements, such as love in a puff vines and seven-son flowers, to give the bouquet movement and interest.

3. Insert the larger focal flowers before the arrangement gets too full. Here, 'Platinum Blonde' and soft pink 'Cafe au Lait' dahlias draw the eye. Working in groups of three to five, nestle these statement blossoms into the foliage base.

4. Layer in a collection of supporting blooms smaller than the main flowers. Erin's bouquet includes 'Kathryn Morley' roses, Scabiosa yellow zinnias, and Collarette dahlias. For the finishing touch, tuck in a few stems of an airy plant to fill out the arrangement—feverfew is a lovely ingredient for this task.

Bountiful
BOUQUETS

Capture the jewels of the garden in idyllic arrangements of flowers and foliage. Each season offers an inspiring array of blooming beauties to fashion into splendid centerpieces for your everyday surroundings.

Celebrate the garden's splendor with captivating displays of your favorite posies. As the first harbingers of spring make their debut, harvest armfuls to bring indoors, where you can savor their beauty in the comfort of your home. Nothing announces the arrival of the season quite like a cheerful assemblage of yellow daffodils and blue grape hyacinths or an assortment of tulips.

With each passing month, the garden offers a limitless array of possibilities for bouquets. Whether you cherish the classic elegance of roses or the charming abundance of 'Lacecap' hydrangeas, you can design an artful arrangement that captures the best of your garden's glory.

Artistry IN BLOOM

Nothing refreshes an interior space more than the presence of fresh flowers.
From delicate posies to grand arrangements, breathe life into your surroundings
with our panoply of ideas for creating and showcasing brilliant bouquets.

An alabaster bouquet adds a grace note of serenity any time of year, left, while a basket of vibrant harvest bounty welcomes autumn, below. Opposite: Celebrate summer with sunflowers. These showy blooms fare best when arranged in a tall vase that can adequately support the heavy blossoms and arching stems. They will last longer when kept hydrated with warm water enhanced with floral food and when displayed in a cool place out of direct sunlight.

A stunning bouquet begins with the freshest blooms. To capture them at their best, harvest when it's cool—in early morning or evening. Look for flowers with firm petals and buds that are just opening, and keep the cuttings hydrated by bringing along a bucket of water to immerse them in immediately after gathering.

Once indoors, select a container that suits the character, scale, and proportion of the blossoms to be placed within. An arrangement of Asiatic lilies might call for an ornate urn, while a casual spray of cosmos may best be showcased in a simple Mason jar. In general, a container that is one-third to one-half the height of the floral display tends to achieve the most symmetrical look. Use taller vases for statuesque beauties, such as gladiolus or bells of Ireland, and shorter ones for medium-stemmed tulips and daffodils.

Opposite: Eggcup collecting (also known as *pocillovy*) has become popular in recent decades. Buds seem to spring from these floral-painted finds—enchanting favors that may prompt recipients to begin quests for their own tiny treasures. This page: A sense of movement draws the eye across this densely packed arrangement.

Fill the container with tepid water, and add floral preservative to lengthen the life of the blooms. Recut the stems with a sharp knife under water just before placing them in the vessel. A slanted cut works best because it allows the stems to better soak up moisture. Be sure to strip off any leaves that will fall below the water line, as they can encourage bacterial growth.

For a casual look that reflects the way flowers grow in nature, select a medley of shapes and sizes. Taller stems, such as delphiniums and penstemons, lend structure and height, while shorter, fuller varieties, including roses, tulips, and lilies, impart a sense of abundance to the overall composition. A well-balanced arrangement benefits from both types of blooms. Add larger flowers first, turning the display as you work, to create a symmetrical look on all sides. Then fill in with the shorter ones.

For a more lush effect, add plants such as baby's breath, feverfew, or Queen Anne's lace to the empty spaces in your bouquet. These light, airy growers create a smooth transition when interspersed among the flowers. Foliage also works well as filler, balancing colorful petals with the serenity of green hues.

To keep the floral display looking its best, place it away from harsh sunlight and drafts created by fans and heating vents. It is important to refresh the water regularly, as needed, and to recut the stems so they can continue to soak up water. With just a little effort, your bouquet will reward you with blooming enchantment for days.

"FLOWERS SEEM INTENDED FOR THE SOLACE OF ORDINARY HUMANITY."

—John Ruskin

A centerpiece can add beauty to an interior, whether it is designed to complement or contrast existing colors. Alabaster roses echo a sitting area's calming shades, below, while pink parrot tulips lend interest to a vignette dressed in blue and white, opposite.

Clockwise from above: Arrangements often make a statement greater than their size, as demonstrated by this posy of pansies. Divided between a pitcher and a collection of glass bottles, fall florals brighten a kitchen counter. A swag of hydrangeas and soft greenery offers the same sentiment as the welcome sign attached to this charming blue door. Opposite: When building a centerpiece that will be viewed from all sides, such as the sumptuous bouquet that tops this entry table, it may be helpful to place the container on a lazy Susan for ease in rotating it as you work. Careful attention ensures there is loveliness to behold from every angle.

Welcome

Setting a floral arrangement before a mirror doubles its impact. Within this elegant gold frame, each shapely leaf, curling tendril, hopeful bud, and blushing petal finds its twin reflected back for all to admire.

*"THE LOVELY FLOWERS
EMBARRASS ME,
THEY MAKE ME REGRET I
AM NOT A BEE."*

—Emily Dickinson

Placing blossoms here and
there throughout the home
allows guests to encounter
unexpected moments of
beauty around every corner.
A lush centerpiece adorns the
dining room table, left, but a
spare cutting enlivens a nearby
gathering spot.

A loosely gathered bundle of fresh-cut finds captures the allure of the cottage garden. Opposite: Greet Easter morning with a glorious wreath that brims with brightly hued blooms. A little bird's nest holds a trio of speckled eggs heralding the season of rebirth.

Creative
CONTAINERS

*When considering how best to showcase
the season's most spectacular blossoms,
choose a charming vessel that will not only
support the structure of the arrangement
but also complement and even enhance the
overall beauty of its presentation.*

Clockwise from above: Bringing a cheerful element to an afternoon of quiet repose is a diminutive bouquet of African violets and other dainties. A loop of ribbon turns a vial of purple blooms into a hanging display, while a gold thimble highlights a single floret of lantana. Opposite: Hollowed-out gourds become organic vases for autumn mums.

Placed along the windowsill, an array of glass bottles of varying shapes and sizes catches the sunlight. Filled with gleanings from a garden stroll, the grouping makes a cohesive statement while also highlighting the loveliness of each posy. Refreshing individual stems as needed adds interest to the assemblage while also, quite literally, extending its shelf life.

Clockwise from left: Slipped over a doorknob, a paper cone filled with yellow tulips offers a cheerful greeting. In this woodland oasis, a moss-covered bench becomes a welcome spot for spotlighting seasonal bounty. A sentimental cache of sterling baby cups filled with tea roses and other pink blossoms gathers on a treasured silver tray. Opposite: To create a centerpiece in a bird cage, fill the vessel that will rest within the enclosure with water, greenery, and a few blooms before securing it inside. Tuck remaining stems into the arrangement from between the wires, creating the impression that the bouquet has grown beyond its borders.

Timeworn earthenware vessels imbue
interiors with classic style. In antique
French terra-cotta pots, brightly hued
Mini Phalaenopsis orchids flourish amid
soft tufts of moss. Opposite: An exuberant
bundle of fruit, flowers, and foliage finds
its equally engaging complement in the
shapely eighteenth-century olive jar that
serves as its basin.

Flowering
BRANCHES

The return of spring stirs sleeping buds from their dormancy, rewarding our winterlong patience with a colorful array of flowers. Bring the beauty inside by creating graceful arrangements composed of fresh-clipped boughs from the garden.

Airy sprays of forsythia, bridal wreath, and
'Lady Banks' roses—along with sprigs of dogwood
and cherry blossoms—adorn a collection of luminous
crystal vases. Mixed with empty vessels and a
smattering of additional trimmings, the composition
creates a dreamy still life of happenstance.

Freshly cut from the backyard or carefully plucked from the garden, contemplative floral vignettes capture the serenity of spring. From sprawling branches in full flower to the sweet simplicity of a single bloom, the bounty of the season brings beauty to any setting. The arrangements can be delicate, as shown left and below, or voluminous, as befits the lobby of a grand hotel, opposite.

THE *Loveliest* OF TABLES

Whether pulled from a dinnerware pattern or plucked from the garden, a bevy of blooms turns mealtime into a celebration of beauty. Taking inspiration from botanical bounty, floral settings offer fragrant charm.

Above: Mingling a florist's peonies and cuttings from a garden with wildflowers plucked from a wayside meadow creates a centerpiece that exudes effortless charm. Left: A miniature bouquet brims from Empress Dresden Flowers porcelain, the perfect pattern for blanketing an afternoon tea in spring's splendor. Opposite: Blue-and-white beckons guests to the table, greeting them with Asiatic Pheasant teacups and saucers. Vibrant shades of red and orange provide a breathtaking complement to the cool tones, while fresh fruit and handwritten recipes stir thoughts of mouthwatering fare.

Schumann-Bavaria china sets the tone for a springtime party centered around a lush arrangement echoing the porcelain's painted motifs. Opposite: Marigold Living linens, with their elaborate design of hand-blocked vines and florals, are the ideal backdrop for showcasing Herend Green Chinese Bouquet tableware and a bevy of lush blooms.

*"FLOWERS ALWAYS MAKE
PEOPLE BETTER, HAPPIER,
AND MORE HELPFUL;
THEY ARE SUNSHINE,
FOOD, AND MEDICINE
FOR THE SOUL."*

—Luther Burbank

Opposite and this page, left: A lovely assemblage of collected china from Vintage English Teacup adds charm to an outdoor table. Atop the linens and lace, a Royal Albert teapot in the Lady Carlyle pattern doubles as a flower vase. Above and below: Whether a gathering is decorated with relaxed woodland fare or the gilded grandeur of a candlelit dinner, an arrangement of blossoms instantly heightens the dining experience. For a nature-inspired bouquet, consider adding a few stems of ornamental kale or cabbage, or let the charm fall where it may with handfuls of petals tossed here and there for a sprinkling of radiant color.

A *Pocket*
FULL OF POSIES

While it's true that flowers are beautiful, there's
more than meets the eye. Beyond the pretty
petals, they speak a language all their own,
and one California florist's tiny bunches
of blooms capture this unique patois
in a most meaningful way.

The idyllic community of Bonny Doon—a place every bit as picturesque as its Scottish name suggests—nestles on a gentle slope near Santa Cruz, California, with redwood forests above and coastal grasslands below. With plenty of sunshine, a temperate climate, and salt-tinged breezes drifting up from the nearby Pacific Ocean, it could easily be mistaken for paradise, which explains the Eden-like garden of floral designer Teresa H. Sabankaya.

Born and raised in East Texas, Teresa's voice still carries a faint drawl, as she points out some of the lovely things blooming in her yard. Though she worked in corporate travel before having children, she was eager to spread her wings when her youngest daughter started preschool. "I had read the *Victoria* book *A Shop of One's Own*," she explains, "and I wanted to be one of those women who created a job they loved."

Opposite: A sunny spring day calls for a meal outdoors, and this secluded glen, with its canopy of new green leaves, is just the spot to gather. This page, above right: The Sabankayas' home, built in 1938, features a unique castle-style turret.

Every thoughtfully designed posy bears a tag explaining the significance of each ingredient. The nosegay on the right, a gift for "My Sweet Friend," includes soft-pink roses (grace and joy) and sweet peas (blissful pleasure).

a posy for you

Love is Grand

Clematis, *mental beauty*
Scented Geranium, *preference*
Ranunculus, *charming affection*
Sweet Pea, *delicate pleasures*
Oregano, *joy*
Rose, *love, beauty*
Lavender, *happiness*

A POSY FOR YOU

My Sweet Friend

Pink Rose: grace, joy
Sweet Pea: delicate pleasures
Delphinium: well-being
Stock: lasting beauty
Wooly Bush: gentleness
Fern: sincerity
Tweedia: hearts that believe in each other

With her fervor for gardening, Teresa knew the venture would be botanical in nature. In the fall of 1999, she planted six hundred French tulips on pure faith. A year later, she bought a shop, naming it Bonny Doon Garden Company after the verdant area she calls home. Now a studio-based business, her own garden is the source for many of its horticultural components. The job allows her to combine her interest in floral design with her passion for the language of flowers, known as *floriography*. "Floral symbolism is such a part of our history," she says. "It's sad that we've left that behind."

Determined to revive this evanescent custom—while also putting her own style on it—Teresa has brought back the tradition with her signature bouquets, which come with a tag explaining the meaning of each ingredient. These eloquent nosegays have garnered her a loyal following and prompted her to write *The Posy Book*, an illustrated compilation of her accumulated knowledge, including a how-to guide for creating more than twenty sweet arrangements that speak straight to the heart.

"Flowers should evoke emotions, memories, and, most of all, adoration for their ephemeral beauty," she writes. "And when you want to convey a very special message, there is nothing like a posy."

*"FLOWERS AND POSIES
CAN SAY THINGS THAT
OUR WORDS CANNOT."*
—Teresa H. Sabankaya

CREDITS & RESOURCES

The Art of Flowers
Editor-in-Chief: Phyllis Hoffman DePiano
Editor: Jordan Millner
Managing Editor: Melissa Lester
Associate Editor: Karen Callaway
Assistant Editor: Leslie Bennett Smith
Art Director: Tracy Wood Franklin
Stylist: Melissa Sturdivant Smith
Editorial Assistant: Kassidy Abernathy
Creative Director/Photography: Mac Jamieson
Photographer: Stephanie Welbourne Steele
Senior Copy Editor: Rhonda Lee Lother
Senior Digital Imaging Specialist: Delisa McDaniel

CONTRIBUTING WRITERS
KAREN L. DARDICK: pages 46 and 49–50
JEANNE DELATHOUDER: pages 52, 54, and 57
KATE CARTER FREDERICK: pages 13–14, 16–17, 21, 24, 26, 58, 60, and 63
KIMBER MITCHELL: pages 75, 77, 82, 85–86, 89–90, 105, 107, 111, and 114

CONTRIBUTING PHOTOGRAPHERS
JIM BATHIE: pages 15 and 89
GUY BONCHET: page 75
KINDRA CLINEFF: page 85
KIMBERLY FINKEL DAVIS: pages 28, 30, 32, 85, 105, 120, and 122–123
STEPHEN DEVRIES: page 87

WILLIAM DICKEY: pages 83, 138–139, and 143
KRISTINE FOLEY: pages 10, 46, and 49–50
JANE HOPE: pages 8, 12–31, 35–38, 78, 89, and back cover
CORINNE JAMET: pages 111 and 127
GEORGIANNA LANE: pages 6–7, 10–11, 14, 21–22, 24, 26, and 98–103
JOHN O'HAGAN: pages 104, 112, 120, 124–125, and 140–141
PIERRE NICOU: page 146
TOSHI OTSUKI: pages 17, 74, and 76–77
KATE SEARS: pages 2, 68–73, 82, 86, 89, 91, 142, and 164
EDOUARD SICOT: pages 47, 49, and 89
MARCY BLACK SIMPSON: Front cover and pages 4–5, 10, 14, 18–21, 23, 25, 27, 29–32, 48, 51–57, 64–67, 79–82, 85–86, 89–90, 92–93, 94–96, 104, 106–108, 110, 121, 128, 131–134, 136, 146–149, and 152–161
MICHAEL SKOTT: page 74

CONTRIBUTING STYLISTS
SIDNEY BRAGIEL: page 147
MISSIE NEVILLE CRAWFORD: pages 48, 51, 64, 66–67, 86, 104, 106–107, and 128
MARIE-PAULE FAURE: pages 111, 127, and 146
MARY LEIGH FITTS: page 85
YUKIE MCLEAN: pages 28–32, 82, 86, 104–105, 112, 120, 122–123, 138–139, 143, 146, and 148
TERESA H. SABANKAYA: pages 154–161
KATHLEEN COOK VARNER: pages 82 and 86

WHERE TO SHOP & BUY

Below is a list of properties and companies featured in this book.

Pages 6–7, 11, and 22: For information on visiting the David Austin Roses Garden Centre in Albrighton, England, see davidaustinroses.co.uk. David Austin Roses, Ltd., 15059 State Highway 64 West, Tyler, TX, 800-328-8893, davidaustinroses.com/us.

Pages 28–29: Similar Carolina Elizabeth oil paintings available at carolinaelizabeth.com. Mayflower Wallpaper: Marble Floral MF10001; 401-824-6968, mayflowerwallpaper.com.

Page 29: Burleigh Pottery: Pink Asiatic Pheasants Teacup and Saucer; +44 1773 740740, burleigh.co.uk.

Page 32: To explore artisan Stephanie Monahan's range of papers, craft supplies, and other wares, visit her website, monahanpapers.com.

Pages 34–39: Iford Manor, Bradford-on-Avon, Wiltshire BA15 2BA, +44 1225 863146, ifordmanor.co.uk.

Pages 40–43, 45: Anna Weatherley Designs: Botanical Art Dinner Plate, similar styles available, Tulip Ruffled Cachepot, similar styles available; annaweatherley.com.

Pages 58–63: Special thanks to the Dahlia Society of Alabama, dahliasocietyofalabama.org, and The American Dahlias Society, dahlia.org.

Page 64: For more information about embroiderer Elisabetta Sforza, visit her website, elisabettaricami .blogspot.com.

Pages 64 and 67: Taylor Linens, 951-296-3530, taylorlinens.com.

Page 65: Gien: Millefleurs Dessert Plate, Millefleurs Tablecloth; gien.com.

Pages 68–73: Special thanks to Carolyn Aiken, warrengrovegarden.blogspot.com.

Pages 98–103: To learn more about Erin Benzakein and her organic flower farm, visit floretflowers.com.

Pages 154–161: To learn more about Teresa H. Sabankaya and her work, visit teresasabankaya.com and bonnydoongardenco.com.

"*FLOWERS REWRITE SOIL, WATER, AND SUNSHINE INTO PETAL'D POETRY.*"

—Terri Guillemets